First Published 1999 by:

STRI, ST. IVES ESTATE, BINGLEY, W
ENGLAND

COPYRIGHT © THE SPORTS TURF RESEARCH INSTITUTE 1999

All rights reserved. No part of this publication may be reproduced, stored in a retrieval system or transmitted, in any form or by any means, electronic, mechanical, photocopying, recording or otherwise, without the prior permission of the copyright owner.

ISBN: 1 873431 44 9

JOINT FOREWORD

Through our Senior Ecologist, Bob Taylor, STRI has been keen to promote environmental awareness among golf course owners and managers, as well as other amenity land users. Although Bob Taylor's main role is giving on-site advice to golf course managers about the whole range of environmental issues on golf courses, he also devotes a significant portion of his time to dissemination of information through talks and publications.

His first book, *A Practical Guide to the Ecological Management of the Golf Course*, gave a general overview of the problems facing golf course managers. This was followed by *Studies in Golf Course Management: No.1 Heathland/Moorland Management.* His third book concerning nest boxes is produced in response to the needs expressed by golf course managers. It is very much a "how to" practical guide, and for nest box construction the excellent diagrams enable even a relatively inexperienced person to tackle some of the simpler designs. As well as construction details, information is also given on siting, maintenance and conservation/golf interest. The book concludes with case studies which provide examples of how the introduction of a successful nest box programme on the golf course actually works in practice.

I commend the publication to all those interested in conservation on the golf course and especially to those interested in encouraging native bird and mammal populations.

Dr Mike Canaway, Chief Executive, STRI

We are delighted to have been invited to support this publication. The Plant Breeding Industry has come under severe criticism in respect of the adoption of modern biotechnology techniques and the impact on the environment. Plant breeders care passionately about the environment. Their whole activity is based on improving that which nature has provided.

In some small way therefore our support to this publication aims at improving the arboreal habitat in and around the golf course and, hopefully, elsewhere. We hope that golf course designers, managers and greenkeepers will take this valuable information and act upon it to increase nesting opportunities and then regularly review their plans to improve both the environment and pleasure for golfers.

We also encourage a proactive approach and hope that golf club members around the country can be involved in this initiative.

Christopher Green, Managing Director, Semundo Limited

ACKNOWLEDGEMENTS

This, the second publication in the series of studies in golf course management, has been long awaited by many golf greenkeepers and golf club manager wishing to contribute to enhancing the wildlife potential of their golf course. For the first time an easy to follow series of drawings outlining the construction through to final assembly, together with accompanying descriptive text, has been produced for golf and other amenity turf users. A range of box types has been included suitable for a wide variety of mammal and bird species.

I am particularly indebted to Semundo Limited for sponsoring the production of the publication. This represents a further indication of the awareness of individuals and companies alike in realising the importance of wildlife conservation and the need to safeguard our future wildlife.

I am also grateful to the design skills of Phil Mason of Design Services for producing the illustrations and to Jonathan Hart-Woods and Margaret Richards for their contribution to the text.

I am especially indebted to Ann Bentley for her help and support in the preparation of this booklet. Her dedication, skill and patience on the desktop publishing system have once again been invaluable.

Bob Taylor, B.Sc. Hons., Senior Ecologist, STRI

CONTENTS

Page

Section I

Introduction 6

Section II. Nest Boxes

Birds 14
Mammals 38
  Badgers 38
  Harvest mouse 40
  Dormouse 42
  Hedgehogs 44
  Bats 46

Section III. Case Studies

Ipswich Golf Club 52
Rudding Park Golf Club 60
Loch Lomond Golf Club 64

Section IV

Appendix 68
References and Useful Contacts 69

Section I

Introduction

Introduction

One of the most obvious aids to wildlife in any situation must be the nest box. Often overlooked, even the most apparently simple garden box design, initially an amusement – an extension of the need to own exotic wildlife, is fast becoming an increasingly important aspect of wildlife conservation. As more and more habitat is lost through modification or total destruction, i.e. for housing, industry, farming, etc., the need for habitat creation increases. Wildlife will, if they are to maintain population numbers, need to become increasingly dependent upon artificial habitats, including the provision of appropriate artificial nesting facilities. It is not just through eccentric quirks of nature that we can find blackbirds nesting within the workings of golf course machinery or great tits nesting in overcoat pockets, it is a strong indication of the obvious lack of suitable natural or semi-natural habitat.

There can be few better areas to target than the golf course. It is often very apparent whilst walking around a given course that although there are many trees, there are frequently very few nests within them. This may in part be due to too few trees planted too widely apart and the underlying field layer managed too intensively (amenity plantations). It may be that the trees themselves lack maturity and so provide very few natural nesting locations. Over-tidying within woodlands or the felling of dead or dying trees will reduce the potential habitat available for birds, bats or other mammals in which to seek refuge.

Even on the "more mature", well established golf courses, the woodlands and trees may lack a strong understorey component (natural shrub regeneration within the lower canopy). This layering, or "structural diversity" as it is often termed, is vital if breeding and feeding facilities are to be encouraged. Without this, the breeding and nesting potential will be reduced considerably.

The above problems are likely to be further obviated once a course adopts a nest box programme and notices the sudden substantial uptake in their use. This may occur in a very short space of time, as at Rudding Park, for example, near Harrogate (see Case Studies). In just one year 88% of the woodpecker nest boxes installed were accepted and occupied. Levels of uptake will give an indication of likely saturation levels which in turn will be largely dictated by total area and quality of habitat available. Levels of uptake may be higher in poorer habitats given very few suitable nesting sites. Availability of appropriate food sources, however, will influence actual levels of saturation. In better quality habitats, whilst there may be an improved food resource, levels of uptake within nest boxes may not be so high due to the presence of naturally occurring nesting features (habitat).

Sensible habitat management is therefore essential if any nest box programme is to be successful. Creating the right (optimum) habitat conditions must remain the first priority. There will be very little merit in encouraging nesting birds if the available food source is insufficient to meet demand and if this is unable to satisfy the likely increase in population size. Similarly, the survival rate of particular species may be severely compromised if the habitat type is barely large enough or sufficiently diverse to sustain a viable population of a given species.

Sustained ecological management will include woodland copse and tree management, grassland management to include grading the rough so as to maximise feeding, hunting, vantage and breeding. A major component of this work must be to maximise structural diversity, i.e. through the development of a range of different age groups within any vegetation type so generating different levels of maturity. Integral here will be the need to create a stratified structure, for example the field, understorey, canopy and high canopy layers, within a given woodland so as to maximise available area for niche colonisation. Species diversity may be important particularly in certain woodlands and in areas of wild flower grassland so as to increase, either directly or indirectly, the total food resource available. Leaving areas situated out of play uncut will help to provide habitat for overwintering. This will be particularly important for insects and small rodents.

Communication

From the above, it is clear that the wildlife benefits of artificial nesting facilities will be greater on golf courses supporting little "natural", i.e. mature and well established, habitat. On courses supporting a good habitat structure, i.e. dead standing trees, older trees, etc., uptake is likely to be reduced.

Artificial nest boxes, however, do have a secondary function and one of considerable importance. Their role in encouraging discussion and communication through the golfing members cannot be over-emphasises. The erection of a series of bat boxes or individual bird boxes will stimulate discussion and hopefully encourage a greater awareness and interest from the membership with regard to wider environmental issues such as tree management (tree felling) work, the reasoning behind allowing the rough grassland to extend out from the woodland edge (ecological corridor habitat), etc.

Having considered the basic ecological theory pertaining to management, it will be possible to focus on the various aspects of nest box construction, siting, erection and maintenance. Possibly, the first question at this stage must be, What species am I likely to attract and which species are most desired?

Species listing

The first step in considering initiating a nest box programme will be to determine through recording what bird species are likely to be encountered on the course. These may range from the resident and common blackbird, robin and blue tit to the much rarer or very occasional sightings of the whitethroat, redstart or nuthatch. Having produced a detailed list over a minimum twelve month period, it will then be necessary to determine which species are likely to reside on the course. A number of those recorded may be occasional or very occasional visitors passing over the course, i.e. summer or winter migrants, the latter arriving on the course for the duration of the colder winter period but returning to other established breeding grounds for the summer.

Around sixty bird species are known to use artificial nesting sites, these include the most obvious blue tit, great tit, robin, wren, etc. through to the less obvious species such as green, great or lesser spotted woodpeckers, nuthatch, spotted flycatcher, tawny and barn owl and kestrel. All of these will, if seen on the course, add considerably to the pleasure of playing a round of golf. The bird song and obvious presence of these birds will enforce the perception of play in an apparently very natural countryside location. From the outside of the course, such work may help to alleviate somewhat the public criticism and concerns often directed at golf towards the relatively selfish use of the landscape resource.

Mammalian populations should also be ascertained. Local Bat Groups and Naturalists Trusts would certainly be worth contacting for possible information. Road casualties will also help to give good information as to species likely to be found on the course. Failing the above, the STRI would be pleased to provide data and guidance on species present.

Construction

Having determined what birds and mammals are likely to be attracted to the nest boxes, it will be necessary to consider the different types of construction available. These are outlined in Section II.

The basic materials are usually wood though if purchased as new, this can be very expensive. It may be far better for those contemplating larger scale projects to consider using discarded timber from timber merchants, pallets, old floorboards, etc. Almost any type of wood will suffice but some may last longer than others. Reconstituted chipboard and blockboard would not be considered suitable. Birch tends to be relatively soft and, although easy to work, may be relatively short-lived. The type of wood used may, however, be more a reflection of what is readily available rather than what may be most appropriate. To prevent warping, the wood should be over 15 mm thick; this will also help to provide insulation during the early spring period and reduce waterlogging. All of the diagrams outlined in Section II have been designed using stock timber of 200 mm x 25 mm and 175 mm x 25 mm. Thinner timber would require a scaling down of the measurements given.

Terracotta, gas or drainage channel or other plastic piping could be used, cut to length, drilled and provided with a wooden floor and roof so as to provide a conventional type box. Care must, however, be taken when erecting pipes as plastic can heat up rapidly under full sun and may be lacking sufficient insulation during the colder evening period. Piping is particularly effective in the construction of artificial sand martin and kingfisher nest sites.

Other materials could be utilised in nest box construction, these have included inner tubes, tyres, piping and concrete. One must always be aware, however, of the potential problems such as lack of insulation, condensation and increased human attraction when using such materials.

When constructing a wooden box, the grain should run vertically so as to assist water shed. Exposed end grain should be kept to a minimum. This can be achieved by, for example, inserting the floor section into the bottom of the box so as to stop water dripping off the sides. Similarly, consideration should be given to internal drainage via the provision of one or more small holes drilled into the base of the box so as to facilitate removal of any internal water.

Assembly

Use a soft pencil to draw the cutting lines on the timber, cut along each line and arrange, checking that the sizes and shapes are correct. Place the back on its side in a vice or similar holding device and secure the first side using 40-50 mm oval nails. Progress to the roof and floor. If applicable, a rubber hinge between the lid and back will prevent water ingress.

Assembling the cut timber should be done with both glue and either galvanised nails or brass screws. Access into the box will be required for maintenance purposes and should be facilitated using a hinged or removable roof or front. Old tyre inner tubes would provide the cheapest source of hinging and would create attractive and functional flashing between back and top. An overhanging roof will further reduce rain damage. Many different devices can be thought of for securing the lid, but possibly the easiest would be a wire looped around a nail!

Fixing

Correct fixing of the box to its location is critical if the box is not to fall whilst occupied. Boxes nailed to trees must be checked at least annually so as to ensure that the growing tree is not pushing the nail out. Steel nails or screws will rust rapidly and can cause localised damaged to the tree. If nails are to be used, "round heads" are preferred to "ovals" in conjunction with a solid hardwood backboard. This will ensure that the nails are gradually forced outwards as the tree grows.

Other possible methods for tying boxes to trees may include robust rubber banding or wire (rubber insulated), although the latter can, if neglected, cut into the tree restricting tree growth. Binder twine (non-biodegradable) may also suffice but again could kill the tree if neglected. Wedging larger boxes into forks, etc. may be a suitable method, particularly for those types supporting kestrel and owl.

Preservation

Creosote is possibly the cheapest and most effective wood preservative although any wood preservative can be used to treat the outside of any bird box. Do not treat the inside. Creosote is very toxic and lethal to bats and should not be used to preserve bat boxes. Indeed, I would never use this product on any part of a bat box. An untreated softwood bat box may last up to eight years.

Location

It is generally understood that boxes should never be positioned in a due south orientation owing to the intense heat that may beat down on the box throughout a long summer's day. This could indeed kill young nestlings. The main criteria must be to ensure that the box is sheltered from strong sunlight during at least part of the day and sheltered from excessive wind and rain. The main criteria are:–

(a) keep the box out of intensive prolonged sunlight,
(b) keep away from the wettest sides of the tree trunk, and
(c) locate the box away from play to protect birds, bats, etc. and the boxes from stray golf balls.

A preferred orientation may be away from the fairway line in an east through to southeast direction, although the south may be acceptable providing that some shade is afforded by neighbouring trees (see additional notes relating to bat boxes).

Additional shelters can be provided by tilting the box forward slightly so as to protect the entrance hole. Initially, a few boxes should be sited uniformly through a given habitat, building up gradually until a saturation level has been observed. Numbering the boxes will be essential for monitoring occupancy or uptake levels.

Consider erecting boxes at different heights within a given habitat and at slightly different orientations so as to maximise uptake. Do not put boxes too close as this may lead to aggressive territorial behaviour.

The eventual aim must be to achieve a natural level of saturation, leaving just one or two boxes spare in any area. Thus, if all boxes become occupied it will be possible to add one or two more providing that sufficient space is available.

Safety

It is up to both the employer and employees of the golf course to take whatever steps are necessary to ensure their own safety when building, erecting or maintaining nest boxes.

Falls are a major cause of accidents and it is therefore essential that ladders or other forms of scaffold are secure before use. Undue risks should be avoided. Nest boxes need not be installed in areas that are almost totally inaccessible. A few metres above ground level may be sufficient most of the time. Similarly, reasonable care must be taken when working in or near watercourses.

Do not use power tools in precarious or dangerous positions. Exercise care when carrying extended aluminium ladders, particularly within the vicinity of overhead cables.

It is the employer's duty to take account of any perceived risks that are likely to be encountered before undertaking the construction or installation work.

Ladders should be secured by a tie rope or with a base plate. A second person standing at the foot of the ladder will prevent slipping only with ladders less than 6 metres long.

The ladder should extend at least 1 metre beyond the highest rung in use. Tools and the bird box should be carried in such a manner as to free both hands to grip the ladder. Do not climb the ladder unless you can hold on to it.

Ladders should never be supported by their rungs. Set the ladders at a stable angle, i.e. 4 units up to 1 unit out, and, most of all, avoid overreaching.

Cleaning

The nests of many birds and animals are home to a variety of fleas and other parasites. If left intact, they will survive to infest next year's young. By removing old nesting material in October/November this problem can be reduced. Boiling water is as effective a treatment as any and remember to never use insecticides and flea powders as they are harmful to small birds and mammals. Check the nesting sites carefully before winter cleaning as boxes may still be in use as winter roosts.

Section II

Nest Boxes

Nest Box Construction
- Birds
- Mammals

Birds

Type of box: Small hole.

Potential users: Great tit, blue tit, coal tit, wren, starling, pied flycatcher, redstart and tree sparrow. Both great spotted woodpecker and nuthatch will adopt this size box on occasion.

Materials: Sawn softwood, oval nail, brass hinges, hook and eye catch, wood glue.

Construction: Note that stock timber 200 mm x 25 mm and 175 mm x 25 mm have been used in the design of this box.

Variations: Starlings favour aperture sizes of 45 mm; redstart 35 mm; nuthatch 32 mm; wren 30 mm; pied flycatcher, great tit and tree sparrow 28 mm; blue tit and coal tit 25 mm. Great spotted woodpecker will excavate an appropriate-sized hole.

Siting: Pied flycatchers prefer sites in woody glades at medium height. Great tits and blue tits favour medium height in any suitable locations, while coal tits prefer a low situation. If redstarts are present on the course, site boxes on oaks preferably at a medium height on the edge of a woodland. Tree sparrows use nest boxes but are easily disturbed, site medium height along appropriate tree-lined wood edges.

Maintenance: Caution should be exercised when clearing some boxes as wrens and tree sparrows will both use boxes as winter roosting sites. If boxes are not in use, clear between November and January.

Conservation/ Golf interest: Most golfers will be familiar with starling, great tit and blue tit, but perhaps unfamiliar with the coal tit mistaking it for a blue tit. Pied flycatcher and redstart are both summer visitors preferring deciduous woodlands/parklands. Nuthatch is a bird that suffers from a shortage of natural nesting sites. More golfers will have heard the nuthatch's insistent "wi-wi-wi" call than seen it scurrying back and forth along the branches and trunks, unless of course a bird table is provided as the nuthatch is partial to peanuts.

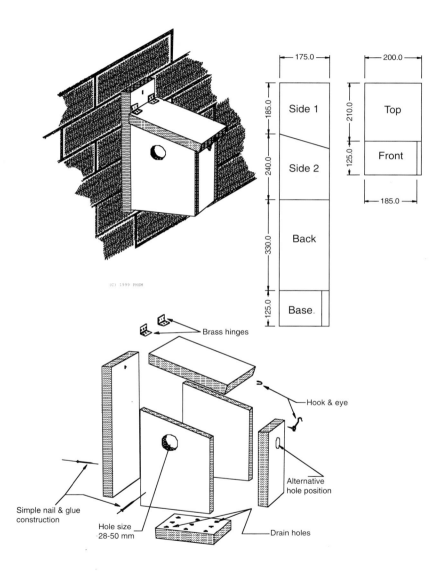

Type of box: Small open fronted.

Potential users: Robin, pied wagtail, spotted flycatcher, pied flycatcher, grey wagtail, dipper and also wren. (The potential use will depend upon a particular bird's distribution.)

Materials: Sawn softwood, oval nails, brass hinges, a hook and eye catch, wood glue.

Construction: Note that stock timber 200 mm x 25 mm and 175 mm x 25 mm have been used in the design of this box.

Variations: By increasing the aperture size for this type of box design, song thrushes, blackbirds and starlings may take advantage and nest.

Siting: For robins/wrens secure the box low in a well camouflaged and well protected area of the course out of range of mis-hit or stray golf balls. Spotted flycatchers prefer nesting sites with shelter above but with a clear outlook at the edge of a glade or fairway. Ivy-clad walls are good sites for both species. Pied wagtails favour low or medium height locations. Walls or bridges close to fairways should yield good results but make sure boxes are not easily detected by ground predators such as rats and weasels, etc. Grey wagtail and dipper may utilise boxes under bridges or close to water.

Maintenance: Clean out and repair as necessary annually between November and January.

Conservation/ Golf interest: Robin and pied wagtail are common on most courses and are identified easily by most golfers. The robin's song is very evocative in spring and autumn. Pied flycatcher and pied wagtail will catch the golfer's eye as they acrobatically hunt insects during the summer months. During winter, large groups of pied wagtails and meadow pipits can be seen on the course searching for food.

Other points: This size box will also attract redstarts on parkland/woodland courses, and dippers on courses with streams and ditches.

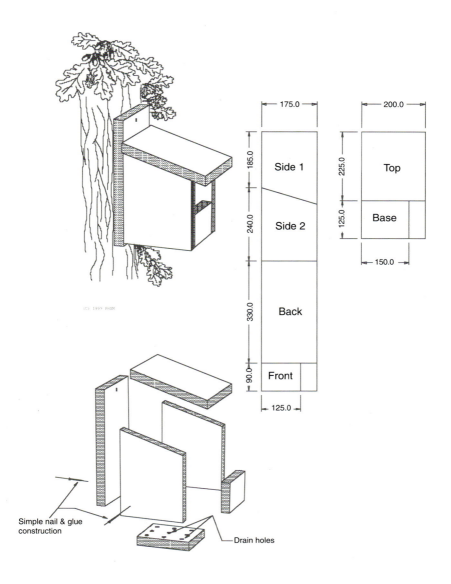

Type of box: Wedge.

Potential users: Treecreeper, coal tit, blue tit and tree sparrow.

Materials: Sawn softwood, oval nails/pin wire, wood glue.

Construction: Note that stock timber 150 mm x 19 mm has been used in the design of this box.

Variations: Aperture size for blue tit and coal tit is 25 mm; great tit and tree sparrow 28 mm; treecreeper prefers 30 mm.

Siting: To attract tree sparrows ensure the box (or boxes as this species will nest communally) is located away from disturbance. Tree sparrows and treecreepers will readily take to boxes sited 3 metres high in trees or occasionally on high walls. Coal, blue and even great tits will nest in boxes sited for tree sparrows and treecreepers.

Maintenance: Tree sparrows will use nest boxes as winter roosting sites so take great care if cleaning out is required. Other nesting species' boxes can be cleaned between November and January but again be careful as wrens will use this size nest box as communal roosting sites in winter.

Conservation/ Golf interest: Golfers are more likely to see most of these birds in winter flocks as they fly from trees and hedges around the course in search of winter food. Coal, blue, great and long-tailed tits are often seen in winter flocks along with goldcrests and treecreepers. The tree sparrow, however, is a nationally declining species (70% in last 25 years), so any tree sparrows using boxes are worth encouraging and safeguarding.

Side view showing top fitting

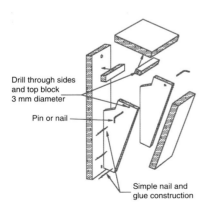

Drill through sides and top block 3 mm diameter

Pin or nail

Simple nail and glue construction

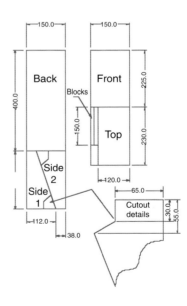

Back

Front

Blocks

Top

Side 2

Side 1

Cutout details

150.0
150.0
400.0
225.0
150.0
230.0
120.0
65.0
30.0
55.0
112.0
38.0

Type of box:	Large entrance.
Potential users:	Jackdaw, stock dove, little owl, great tit, nuthatch and starling.
Materials:	Sawn timber, oval nails, brass hinges, screws.
Construction:	Note that sawn softwood 225 mm x 25 mm and 175 mm x 25 mm have been used in the design of this box.
Variations:	Manipulate the dimensions of the design to attract the different woodpecker species: Great spotted woodpecker – 400 mm x 140 mm with a 50 mm aperture; Lesser spotted woodpecker – 200 mm x 140 mm with a 32 mm aperture; Green woodpecker – 450 mm x 180 mm with a 60 mm aperture.
Siting:	For bird species other than woodpeckers site the box in a position not exposed to wind and rain. Remember best results are achieved when natural sites are in short supply, so look around the course for groups of conifer or recently tidied woodland areas. For great spotted woodpeckers site high on a tree trunk and fill the box with expanded polystyrene or bark chips as they prefer to excavate their own sites. Green woodpeckers prefer sites high up trunks in deciduous woodland. Lesser spotted woodpeckers prefer the underside of a sharply angled branch and filled with wood-chips.
Maintenance:	Clean out and repair as necessary annually between November and January.
Conservation/ Golf interest:	The sociable jackdaw, i.e. the smallest of the British crow family, is often seen in groups foraging along the woodland/fairway edge. The little owl, which can often be seen during the day if disturbed calling "kip-kip-kip" in alarm, is not uncommon on parkland/woodland courses. The woodpeckers will be more often heard by golfers than seen, especially in early spring as they call out to attract mates and establish territories. Most easily identified are the bigger and less secretive green and great spotted woodpeckers as they fly over the course with a distinctive undulating flight pattern. All these species prefer to nest in old trees. Given a shortage of old/mature trees in the UK, nest boxes play an important part in providing suitable alternative sites.

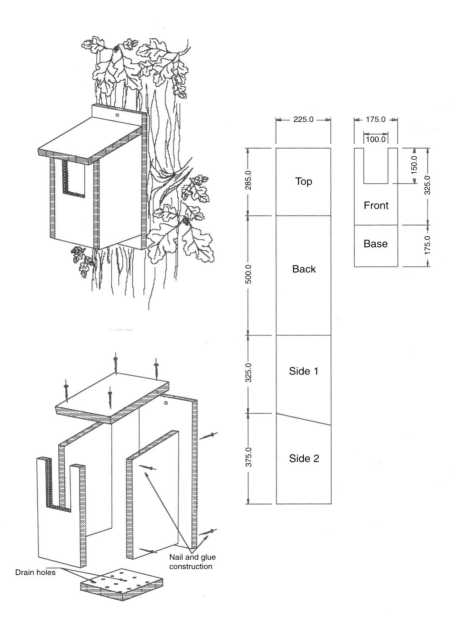

Type of box: Large open fronted.

Potential users: Kestrel, jackdaw, collared dove and little owl.

Materials: Exterior grade plywood (20 mm), oval nails/brass screws, wood glue.

Construction: Note that exterior grade plywood 20 mm thick has been used in the design of this box. The stick/perch along the front of the aperture is very important and should extend a sufficient length beyond the box to allow adults/juveniles to perch with comfort.

Variations: Without the perch, kestrels will be reluctant to nest but all the above species plus possibly blackbirds and starlings will nest happily in well screened boxes of this type.

Siting: For kestrels, high up (at least 5 metres) in a tree or building 3 metres if on an isolated wooden post or steel scaffolding pole concreted into the ground. Because these pole/post boxes are highly visible, it is advisable to locate them in areas of the course where little disturbance will occur.

Maintenance: Clean and repair annually between November and January. It is worth remembering when erected on a pole/post box that for maintenance the construction must take the weight of a person up a ladder.

Conservation/ Golf interest: The collared dove is one of the few success stories in terms of increasing bird populations. Introduced by accident in 1952, it has become widely adaptable in terms of nesting sites. More commonly heard on the golf course than seen given its characteristic "koo-koo-koo" call.

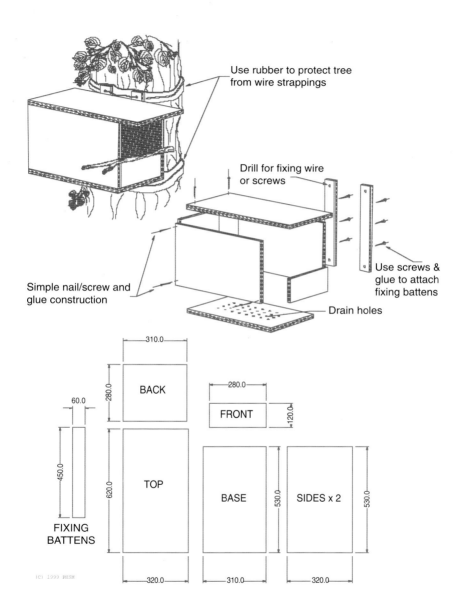

Type of box: Chimney.

Potential users: Tawny owl, kestrel, jackdaw, starling, robin and great tit.

Materials: Sawn softwood, oval nails and U tacks, brass hinges and door catches, metal wire or polythene banding, piece of hose or car tyre placed between tree and wire to prevent damage to the tree.

Construction: Note that sawn softwood 225 mm x 25 mm has been used in the design of this box.

Variations: All the species listed above will take advantage of a chimney box of the above dimensions.

Siting: This box is designed to attract birds which nest in holes created by broken or damaged boughs. The box should be fitted under a bough at about a 45° angle high up.

Maintenance: Clean out and repair where necessary annually between November and January.

Conservation/ Golf interest: The tawny owl is more likely to be heard than seen as it roosts during daylight in tall conifers or dense holly bushes Golfers may hear it twit-twooing at dusk. The kestrel is our commonest bird of prey and is most likely to be seen hunting over the rough grassland of the course. Both birds suffer from a lack of naturally available nesting sites but the kestrel is more adaptable and may well use this box aimed at the tawny owl. Both are spectacular birds to watch hunting.

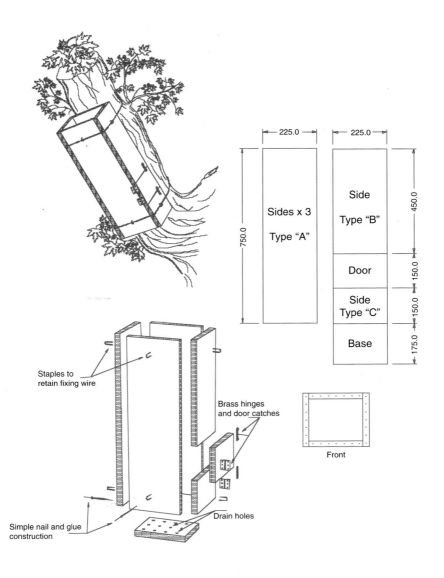

Type of box:	Barn owl box (indoor and outdoor).
Potential users:	Barn owl.
Materials:	*Indoor:* Floor grade chipboard, oval nails or brass screws, wood glue. *Outdoor:* Exterior grade plywood (minimum thickness 19-20 mm).
Construction:	It is important to use the correct materials for outdoor use (exterior grade plywood no less than 19 mm thick). The basic design for both indoor (Figure 2) and outdoor (Figure 3) boxes is the same but if you wish to create two boxes, one for indoor and one for outdoor, construct the pitch roof as illustrated in Figure 3 for external use.
Siting:	Only reasonably quiet and undisturbed buildings around the course close to farmland would be suitable. If you are unsure of barn owl presence in buildings on the course, a deposit of large, black, shiny pellets usually indicates occupancy. Locate the box in a dark corner away from the main entrance. Do not site boxes in buildings close to roads as the barn owl's hunting methods make it vulnerable to collision with cars. It is useful to position both one indoor and outdoor box in the same territory as the barn owl requires both roosting and nesting sites.
Maintenance:	Clean the boxes annually between November and January but make sure the boxes are empty beforehand because the owls will continue to roost in them throughout the winter.
Conservation/ Golf interest:	The barn owl is such a rare breeding British bird today that to have a breeding pair is to have a nesting site of national importance. Despite every effort to stem the decline, barn owl numbers are dwindling and any help with roosting or nesting would be of enormous benefit. Golfers, if they are lucky, will see this large white owl hunting silently at dusk over rough grassland.

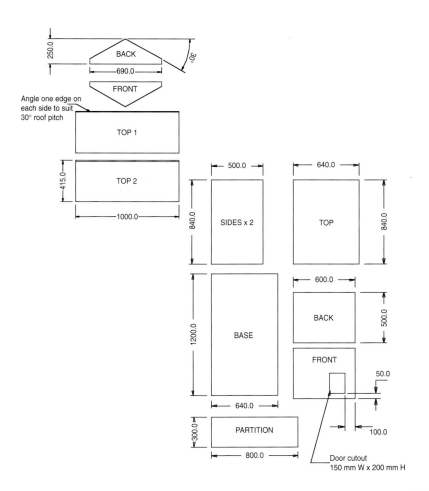

Figure 1

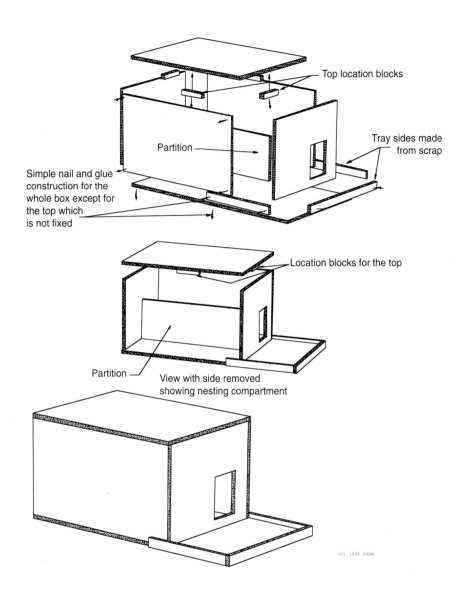

LARGE OWL BOX FOR USE INSIDE (BARNS AND LOFTS, ETC., FLOOR GRADE CHIPBOARD)

Figure 2

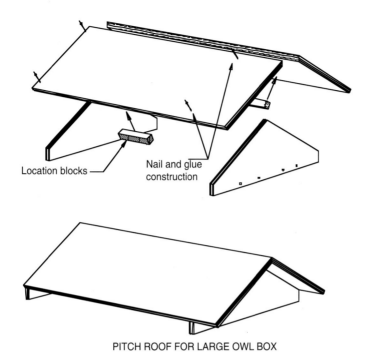

PITCH ROOF FOR LARGE OWL BOX

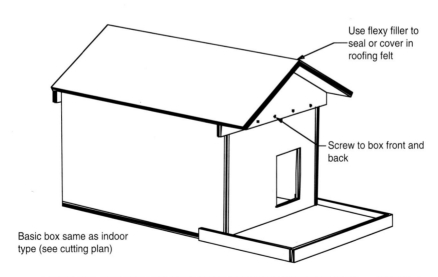

LARGE OWL BOX FOR USE OUTDOORS (EXTERIOR PLYWOOD 19-20 mm THICK)

Figure 3

Type of box:	Swallow nesting platform: Swallow "cup" or "bowl box".
Potential users:	Swallow, house sparrow.
Materials:	*Platform:* Sawn softwood, oval nails, wood glue. *Cup:* Plywood (12 mm), garden wire, coconut shell.
Construction:	*Platform:* Note that stock timber 200 mm x 19 mm will be used in this design. *Cup:* Cut an empty coconut shell in half. Place the cut edge on an appropriately sized piece of 12 mm plywood and draw/mark the position of the shell required for fixing on the board. Mark out and drill the board and coconut shell at 10 mm intervals using a 3 mm drill bit. Using garden wire and pliers, fasten the shell to the plywood plaque, matching the holes in the board and shell at correct 10 mm intervals as per diagram.
Variations:	It is possible that house martins or, more likely, house sparrows will utilise these structures alongside their intended use. A more specific design intended for swallows is also indicated opposite.
Siting:	Swallows prefer to nest on the sides of beams and walls within buildings such as machinery sheds, outbuildings, workshops, etc.
Maintenance:	Swallows will often repair and rebuild old nest sites, so do not clear platforms annually.
Conservation/ Golf interest:	Climate change appears to suggest that swallows are returning for summer in England earlier and departing for Africa sooner than ten years ago. Every assistance in early nesting will be beneficial. Every golf course through the summer will benefit from views of this spectacular summer migrant as it cruises low over fairways or skimming the surface of ponds in search of insect prey. If a house sparrow does take over a platform, rest assured you are still playing an important conservation role as the house sparrow has declined considerably over the last 25 years.

Small hole box with entrance to front. Note damage created possibly by starlings or woodpeckers to enlarge aperture size. A metal plate would prevent this

Clearly labelled wedge with side entrance

Annual monitoring of bat boxes at Rudding Park Golf Club

Starlings can be frequent occupants of nest boxes

Commercially produced box for larger birds of prey, including owls

Dipper box sited under bridge

Roosting site for harvest mice. Novel approach using tennis ball and stake

Dormouse box situated in hazel scrub at Ipswich Golf Club

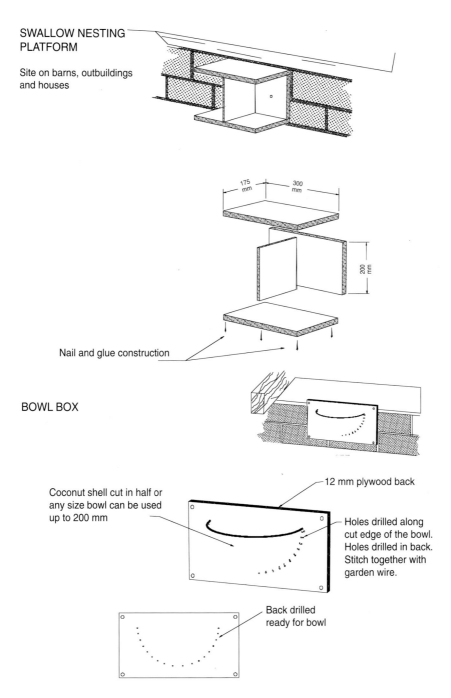

Type of box:	Floating raft.
Potential users:	Grebe, duck, goose, moorhen, coot and black-headed gull.
Materials:	Sawn softwood, polystyrene block, polythene bags/sacks, plastic baking tray or similar, wire, weighting materials, i.e. rubble or concrete (for ballast).
Construction:	Adapt the construction plan opposite to suit the size of your container. Make sure you build in some means of anchoring the platform in your design, i.e. a rope/chain and some form of anchor, to prevent the platform from moving too far. The RSPB Rivers & Wildlife Handbook suggests the following procedure for raft construction:– 1. Construct the frame. 2. Add the platform, floats and fittings. 3. Add soil/gravel/ballast material until the raft floats at the correct level. 4. Anchor in position. Note that stock timber 150 mm x 100 mm and 100 mm x 25 mm have been used in the design of this raft. If you wish to build a more ambitious raft or island, see pages 30-34 of the British Trust for Ornithology's Guide No.23 Nest Boxes by C. du Feu.
Siting:	Best results for this size construction are achieved when the raft or rafts are located in fairly deep water or where the water level tends to fluctuate.
Maintenance:	The raft should be checked and repaired annually. If not required over winter, why not bring it into the machine shop for an overhaul in preparation for spring. Remember to mark the site for relocation with a buoy.
Conservation/ Golf interest:	Many golf courses have ponds and water features too small for islands and therefore no suitable breeding habitat for birds like moorhen, coot and mallard. By locating a floating raft or rafts, this imbalance can be redressed. Any round of golf would be enhanced by members being able to monitor a nesting water bird's progress and the emergence of ducklings/goslings or young coots and moorhens.

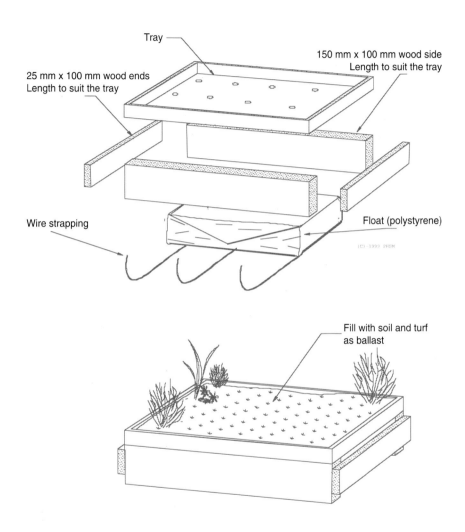

Simple raft

Mammals

Badgers

Legislation

Badgers are given strict protection via the Badgers Act 1992 which basically makes it an offence to disturb a badger whilst occupying a sett, to intentionally damage, destroy or obstruct access to an active sett or to illegally kill, injure, ill-treat or dig badgers from a sett. It is, however, sometimes necessary to discourage badgers from particular areas and creating an artificial sett in an appropriate location may be an ideal way of achieving this. Consult first either English Nature, MAFF or the National Federation of Badger Groups (see References and Useful Contacts) for additional guidance.

Factors to bear in mind when siting an artificial badger sett

- There should be adequate cover in the immediate vicinity of the entrance.
- A natural source of food throughout the whole year.
- A soil which is well drained but firm to prevent collapse. A badger would not use a sett for long without wanting to extend it.
- A source of bedding, i.e. straw, required for prevention of heat loss.

Design requirements

- Tunnel needs to slope upwards towards the chamber to help drainage.
- Sett needs to be well aerated, therefore more than one entrance is needed, preferably at different levels, to allow a flow of air through the system.
- The whole construction needs to be waterproof and consideration will therefore need to be given to appropriate materials, particularly for the roof.

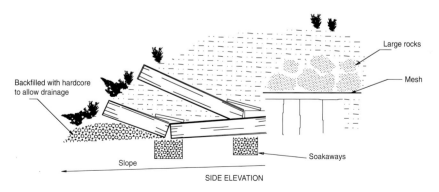

SIDE ELEVATION

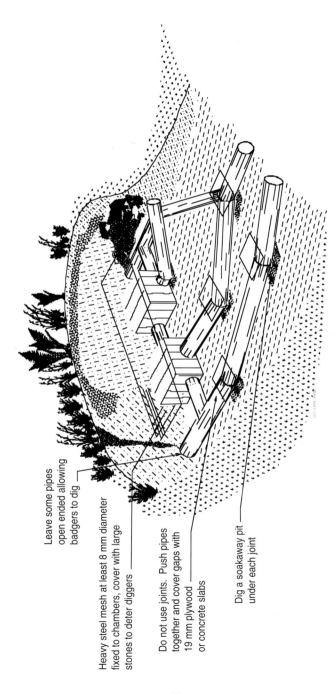

Leave some pipes open ended allowing badgers to dig

Heavy steel mesh at least 8 mm diameter fixed to chambers, cover with large stones to deter diggers

Do not use joints. Push pipes together and cover gaps with 19 mm plywood or concrete slabs

Dig a soakaway pit under each joint

Harvest mouse

Golf courses spread over large tracts of countryside can contribute significantly in improving our knowledge on the distribution and status of harvest mice.

Harvest mice live in taller rough grassland alongside hedgerows, woodland margins, clearings, etc., in bramble, in reed beds, alongside roadside verges and within arable land. Their favourite grasses, apart from wheat, may be common reed (*Phragmites*) and cocksfoot (*Dactylis*) but any thick or dense stand of grass may prove rewarding. The present status of harvest mice remains very patchy and it is thought that populations are declining rapidly, largely through modern methods of agriculture and habitat loss.

In an attempt to study the distribution and ecology of harvest mice, the Imperial College Field Station (1995) has pioneered a particularly novel and successful method of attracting and thus recording the presence or absence of harvest mice within a given area.

Construction

A small 16 mm diameter hole is cut into a tennis ball to act as an entrance. This hole tends to be too small to let any other rodents in but is ideal for harvest mice which weigh little more than 6 grams cf. the wood mouse, 19 grams and the house mouse, 13 grams. A few smaller holes (3-4 mm diameter) should be made in the base of the ball for drainage. One or possibly two balls could be attached to a cane or stake using wire or by cutting slits in the side of the ball, threading the cane through. The height of the balls will be dependent upon their location within any given vegetation.

Location

Harvest mice prefer the denser parts of any vegetation and it is here that the nesting site should be provided. In thick, dense swards of deep rough the balls should be situated towards the top of individual tussocks, i.e. at around 10-15 cm above ground level. Canes could be spaced some 1 metre or so apart.

Timing

Nest balls should be positioned during the early summer period, i.e. May to June, and should contain a small amount of bird seed and hay to encourage uptake. Evidence of activity is usually noted by:–
(a) actual sightings;
(b) a woven grass nest within the tennis ball;
(c) the bird seed being eaten.

Nesting usually occurs between early autumn and late spring.

Records of harvest mice should be forwarded to STRI with a copy to the Mammal Society (address outlined in References and Useful Contacts Section).

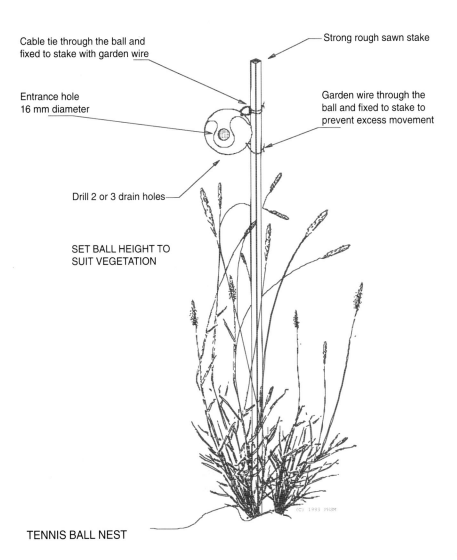

TENNIS BALL NEST

Dormouse

The dormouse is often overlooked due to its nocturnal habit and to the fact that it spends possibly half of the year in hibernation. It apparently has a relatively scattered distribution throughout the UK, being found generally south of a line from the Wash through into parts of Wales, with one or two localised colonies occurring in the Lake District. Dormice prefer good quality deciduous woodlands supporting sufficient food source, including honeysuckle, bramble and hazel. The woodlands need to be relatively dense and dormice are therefore likely to only occur in the older, more mature woodlands on the golf course. Nest boxes for dormice are very similar to those used for birds, except that the box is situated at around 1.5-2.5 metres high and the entrance hole should face the tree. A 20 mm gap will need to be provided between tree and entrance hole.

Construction

The box should be made of sawn, untreated timber 25 mm (1 in.) thick. The box should support a hinged lid so that it can be checked on occasion to assess levels of occupancy and for maintenance. Boxes are best wired to trees so as to facilitate removal and repositioning. Several boxes should be placed in small groups, i.e. in adjacent trees, so as to increase the chance of uptake.

Timing

Construction and erection should take place throughout the winter period, i.e. whilst the mice are hibernating, so as to be ready for use during the spring period.

DORMOUSE BOX

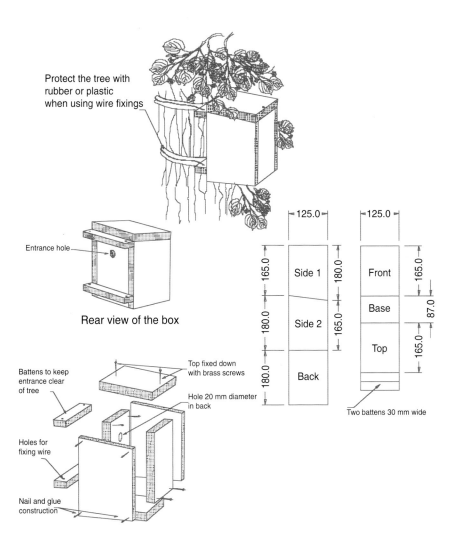

Hedgehogs

Hedgehogs are well established throughout the country and are a very welcome sight on the golf course. Hedgehogs are further advantageous given the regular healthy diet of invertebrate pests, including slugs, earthworms, leatherjackets, etc.

Hedgehogs can be encouraged through the provision of a purpose-made facility.

Construction

One of the main parameters to consider when constructing and siting a hedgehog nesting facility must be that it remains dry throughout the winter period. The box needs to be large enough to support the mammals without causing too much condensation and raised above ground level slightly to reduce rising damp. The artificial box should be covered with soil and dead leaves for further insulation which may also be lined to prevent direct water percolation. A standard type overflow pipe should be included for added ventilation (see drawing opposite).

HEDGEHOG

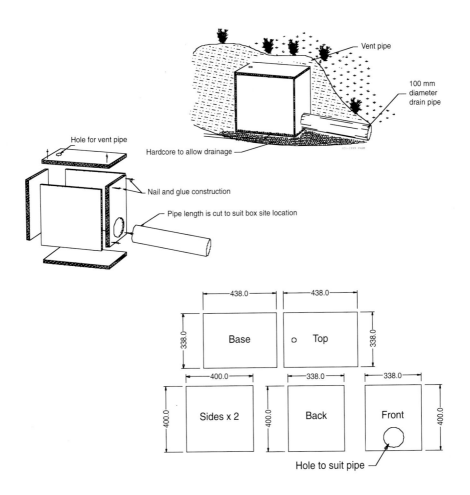

Bats

All of our fifteen native bats are under threat from loss of habitat and suitable sites for breeding, hibernating and roosting. Various factors have contributed to the decline in suitable habitat, including changes in farming methods and policy, loss of semi-natural woodland and the increasing usage of chemicals where bats reside.

The golf course provides an excellent opportunity to slow the speed of their decline through the provision of bat boxes and associated habitat schemes.

It will, however, be of little benefit to erect bat boxes if no further attention is given to developing appropriate rough/habitat quality.

Improving habitat quality will increase the total diversity of insects that the different bats require. The rough, if managed sensibly, can act as an ecological link through the course, providing a safe route of passage for bats both for roosting and feeding. Indeed, such belts of scrub, trees and grassland, i.e. the fairway screens, etc., with extended wood edges are a particularly valuable habitat resource for bats.

A major concern expressed towards amenity management is the constant drive for over-tidying. Whilst on the golf course there will be certain areas that need to readily facilitate ball retrieval, other areas could be left to provide suitable habitat for bats. Hedges too can provide an excellent habitat resource, particularly for our smallest bat, the pipistrelle, which can often be seen flying around the taller unkempt hawthorns just before nightfall during the summer months. Water features too can be particularly important for the daubentons bat which can infrequently be seen flying low over the water's surface like a swallow or swift in search of insects. The noctule is our largest bat and is commonly seen during the summer flying high over water bodies in search of air-borne insects rising on the thermals. Hedging and marginal planting around water features is of major importance here.

The majority of bats likely to be encountered on the golf course will probably prefer to roost, breed and hibernate in the cracks and crevices of old trees rather than, as so often thought, in caves or other familiar dwellings. Given the marked lack of older trees on so many golf courses, particularly newly constructed ones on farmland sites, bat boxes can contribute significantly to their conservation. Eleven of our fifteen bats will use nest boxes for roosting and mating, six species are known to use bat boxes for breeding.

Consideration should be given to providing both summer and winter boxes, these being attached in pairs or even threes around a given tree.

Summer boxes need to be sufficiently large so as to allow a maternity colony to cluster and conserve heat and so keep the young warm.

These may be used throughout the year, except in particularly cold weather conditions, normally below -4°C. The summer boxes are best placed where bats are known to feed but with few potential roosts. Individual boxes should be placed as high as possible in sheltered, wind-free areas that benefit from at least some sun for part of the day. A suitable flight path needs to be maintained to allow bats easy access to and from the boxes.

Winter boxes, also called hibernation boxes, are important in maintaining the bat populations throughout the winter months. These need to provide sufficient insulation during adverse winter weather conditions. To satisfy these criteria, boxes need to be much thicker than the summer boxes, 100 mm thick planking is an option, or alternatively constructed with an inner and outer layer separated by insulating material. Winter boxes are often constructed out of hollowed-out logs with suitable planking to the top and bottom. All boxes should be well built, dry, rainproof and draught-free. The wood used should be no less than 25 mm thick, rough cut on all surfaces, with an entrance slit underneath of between 15 and 20 mm wide. Ideally, the box should be about 100 mm from back to front, between 100 and 300 mm high and between 100 and 150 mm wide. Larger boxes should not be built as these may not generate sufficient warmth. The boxes should ideally be placed as high as possible in established trees, leaving a nominal 1 metre above the box clear of obstruction and a nominal 3 metres in front to facilitate access.

Further information on bat boxes can be obtained from the Bat Conservation Trust (see References) or from *Bat Boxes: A Guide* produced by R.E. Stebbings and S.T. Walsh available through the Bat Conservation Trust.

A number of suppliers can supply ready-made bat boxes with booklets on siting, these include Batalogue, c/o Bat Groups of Britain (Sales), 10 Bedford Cottages, Great Brington, Northampton, NN7 4JE and World of Difference, 14 Woburn Walk, London, WC1. Cement and sawdust boxes with siting information are available through Jacobi, Jayne & Co, Hawthorn Cottage, Maypole Hoath, Canterbury, Kent, CT3 4LW.

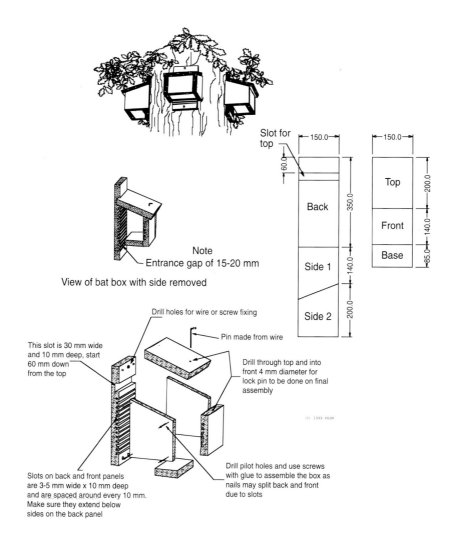

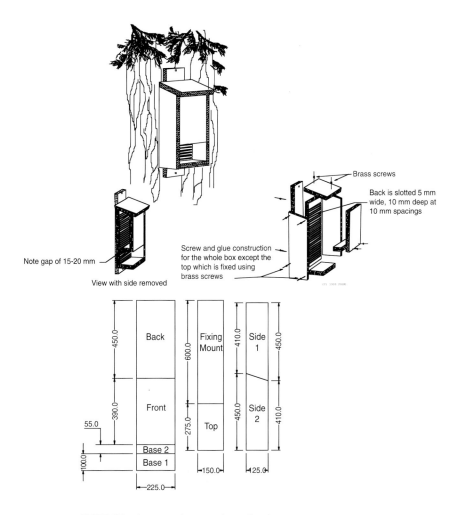

NOTE: Wood must not be treated or painted

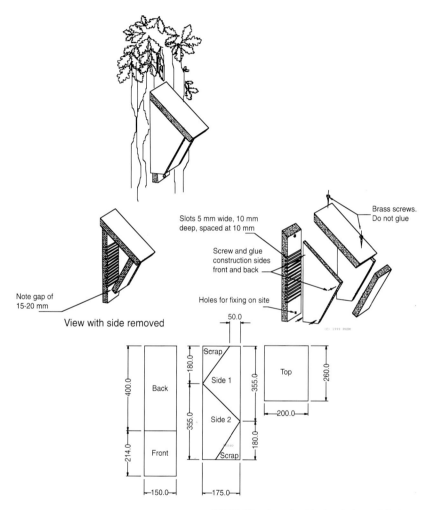

NOTE: Wood must not be treated or painted

Section III

Case Studies

- Ipswich Golf Club
- Rudding Park Golf Club
- Loch Lomond Golf Club

Nest Box Scheme at Ipswich Golf Club: A Case Study
By Neil Sherman

Construction

Nest boxes were first erected at Ipswich Golf Club in 1991.

The types of boxes to be made in the first year were decided on by consulting the bird species list of the course and noting which would use boxes. The success of the different boxes was used to gauge subsequent types to build. Construction usually took place in the quieter winter months of the working year. In general, 18 mm exterior marine plywood was used for the main "box", the roof being fixed with a hinge of plastic flashing material and held secure with a latch. Metal plates with circles of various sizes (25 mm, 28 mm, 30 mm and 32 mm) were put over the holes cut in the front of the boxes to help prevent predation. A number was painted on the bottom of each box to help in location.

Bird box types included:–

> 25 mm hole – Blue tit
> 28 mm hole – Great tit
> 30-32 mm hole – Tit
> Large open front
> Small open front
> Treecreeper
> Owl
> Kestrel
> Woodpecker

Positioning

All boxes were put up in the winter to give the birds time to acclimatise to them. To scatter the boxes over the site, a tit box was placed near each of the holes on the 18 hole course. Some were put in trees on the edge of fairways so as to be in view of the players and thus highlight the work being done. Others were positioned just off the playing areas and the rest along the designated nature trails on the site.

Each box was put in a tree on the shady side (between northwest and southeast) to protect the young from hot sun, wet southwesterly winds with thought also given to damage through golf balls! All those in clear view were erected at least 2 metres high to stop attacks from ground level predators (but boxes in more hidden locations were placed lower). The open-fronted boxes were put in trees with a good growth of ivy to try and hide them from the resident grey squirrels and hopefully attract the spotted flycatchers which had nested in this type of cover naturally in previous years.

The tree creeper boxes were put up either on tall straight trunks or underslung on large overhanging limbs to try and match their natural nesting sites of cracks and fissures in bark.

The more specialist, larger boxes were positioned very carefully in or close to habitat where the target species occurred. The two owl boxes were placed in secluded woodland – one in an area of pines and a second in an oak within the mature deciduous wood in the middle of the site. Both were erected at least 5 metres high, wedged in large forks in the tree canopy. Tawny owls were known to be present near both locations.

The kestrel box was positioned again at 5 metres, plus in a large oak tree on part of the heathland to the edge of the course. Farmland and an adjacent heathland site (Purdis Heath) fringe this location. Kestrels were often seen hunting in this area, coming in from the farmland. Access to the box entrance was cleared to allow the birds a clear view of it.

A woodpecker box was secured 5 metres up a large sycamore on the edge of the central woodland, again in a location where woodpeckers were frequently seen and heard. It was placed well away from the playing areas to prevent disturbance and, once in position, was filled with large blocks of balsa wood to allow the woodpeckers to 'tunnel' onto the interior of the box to form their nest.

After each box was erected, the number was recorded along with a brief description of its site, e.g. Box 3 – left of 10th tee. The month and year were also noted to keep track of how long the box had been up (see results section).

Monitoring

To find out if the boxes are being used, during the spring and early summer (April to July) they are watched for five minutes through binoculars (to prevent disturbance). The adults, if young were present, would show themselves very quickly. On occasions, the young themselves could be heard. Using the list of box locations which was drawn up at the beginning of the scheme, the species using each box was recorded. One visit each month was found to be sufficient to record something of note for most boxes. The owl boxes were not checked in this way for the obvious reason – they are nocturnal!

Box inspection

Checking the boxes does not occur until late in the year, normally after the first frosts. The birds would have finished using them at this time. Also, any parasites present in the old nests (fleas, lice, etc.) should have been killed off by the cold weather, making inspection a much more bearable exercise for whoever has to do it! Long gauntlets are still used as some parasites may persist.

The procedure used at the Golf Club involves finding each box again with reference to the list drawn up at the beginning of the survey (see box positioning section). The nest box is then checked for damage, any repairs required being noted down. The box is opened carefully in case anything is attached to the lid (e.g. wasp's nest, spiders, etc.). If a bird's nest is present, it is first checked for any remaining eggs or young which have died during nesting. This will help in identifying the species that used the box if they were not recorded during the summer. Anything unusual or significant is similarly noted down. Numerous species of insect and other life have been hibernating in the boxes, including hoverflies, hornets and a peacock butterfly.

The types of nest found in boxes at Ipswich Golf Club are:–

Tit nests   Blue, great, coal and marsh tit nests all tend to consist of a moss base built up with hair or feathers, although in the case of the coal tit pine needles may be found as it is associated with conifer trees.
Again consists of mosses, hair and feathers but is much smaller than tit nests (about fifty percent).

Robin   Made mostly of leaves and twigs formed into a domed shape.

Spotted flycatcher   Again mostly of leaves but does not form a dome, more of a shallow saucer.

Nuthatch   Mainly formed from chippings of bark. The entrance hole of the box is plastered with mud so that only the nuthatch itself can enter.

As much of the old nest material as possible has to be removed to prevent the build up and spread of parasites to the next set of users. After cleaning, the box is closed and resealed with the catch before moving on to the next one.

The owl boxes are also included at this time but not touched after December as tawny owls start nesting in January/February. They are notoriously territorial, so a colleague is always present during inspection to warn of any approaching owl! (Remember, owls fly silently due to their specialist wing feathers.) They make no nest as such but if the box has been used there will be a strong smell coming from the pellets and droppings at the base of the box.

Once all the boxes have been examined, those requiring it are repaired and returned to their locations. The most common form of damage at Ipswich Golf Club comes from woodpeckers which drill holes into the box bases to obtain the eggs and young (part of their staple diet). Prior to the fitting of metal plates around the entrance holes of tit boxes, nuthatches would often double the diameters overnight. Only very occasionally do golf balls cause problems – trying to score a birdie perhaps!

Tabulating the results

All the information gathered during the summer observations and the winter inspection is collected and put into a table of results using the following headings:–

YEAR	1995
NUMBER OF BOX	58
TYPE OF BOX	28 mm
LOCATION	Back Right 17th Green
DATE PUT UP	February 1992
SUCCESS	Yes
SPECIES	Blue tit
OTHER USERS OF NOTE	Hoverflies (2)

Here is an example of how the results are used at Ipswich Golf Club once the yearly table is complete:–

Nest box Survey 1995

Boxes in use (number in good order on course) = **62**

Boxes actually used during year = **42**

Percentage used $\frac{42}{62} \times 100$ = **68%**

Now using the total number of boxes used by birds (total 42), it is possible to find out what percentage of this total was used by each species. So:–

Blue tits	**31 Boxes**
Great tits	**7 Boxes**
Spotted flycatchers	**2 Boxes**
Jackdaws	**1 Box**
Owls	**1 Box**

Each of these figures is divided by the total number of boxes used by birds, e.g.

$$\text{Blue tit} \quad \frac{31}{42} \times 100 = \mathbf{74\%}$$

$$\text{Great tit} \quad \frac{7}{42} \times 100 = \mathbf{18\%}$$

And so on.

These percentages are then used to produce a pie chart for display at the Golf Clubhouse for members to see the results for the year.

Comments on the results

(a) Position of the box in relation to species using it. Position will affect which bird will use a box. Spotted flycatcher will use boxes positioned in a large silver birch tree partially concealed by ivy (*Hedera helix*). This is exactly the condition the birds require to nest naturally.

Positioning is **not** a major factor for blue or great tits. In these cases the size of the entrance hole (25 mm or 28 mm) is paramount in deciding which species will occupy the nest box.

(b) Seasonal variations in climate. The period from the summer of 1995 to the late autumn of 1996 was one of the driest recorded at Ipswich Golf Club. Less than 10 inches (250 mm) fell between 1 November 1995 and 1 November 1996. This had an obvious knock on effect to the bird populations. Dry weather means less soft-bodied insects to feed the young which will cause an abnormal mortality rate. The problems of the 1996 spring were further compounded by generally low temperatures and a run of 'late' frosts. This meant that emerging insect populations were up to three weeks behind average (borne out by regular moth survey records for the site). Thus, some adults failed to forage enough food to sustain hatching young. Evidence to support this can be gleaned from the results. In 1994, an average year, 75% of the bird boxes put up were used (64% by blue tits). In 1996 however, this had dropped to 71% (only 56% by blue tits) and several of these nests contained either dead eggs (Nos. 8 and 24) or dead young (Nos. 14, 22 and 49). A similar sort of effect can be expected if the spring is wet; birds lose feeding time and struggle to find enough food to rear a full brood of chicks. This effect has yet to be seen during the survey at Ipswich Golf Club.

In the long term, numbers recover back to 'normal' levels as this is all part of the natural fluctuation in populations.

(c) Box predation. Limited success of the large open-fronted boxes was noted, possibly due to the presence of the grey squirrel, a notorious predator of eggs and young birds. Any nests built in these boxes are sadly easily accessible to the squirrels and consequently there are no plans for further boxes of this type to be erected on the site. The use of metal plates on the front of all 'tit' boxes has been totally successful in stopping predation by squirrels, etc. Instead, they are unfortunately attacked from beneath by woodpeckers which drill a hole through the base and extract the eggs that way. Making the bottom of the boxes previously attacked from a thicker piece of timber (25-30 mm) has subsequently deterred them.

(d) Interesting nest material. In 1994, one of the boxes used by blue tits was found to contain long white hairs which were later confirmed as belonging to horse or pony. About half a mile from the bird box on the edge of the golf course by the main car park is a small paddock with a white pony! It would appear the birds had travelled all that distance to collect suitable nesting material, which gives some idea how far these birds can range in their lifetime.

In 1996, a box was used by great tits, the adults having been observed entering during the summer. When inspected in the autumn, the nest consisted mainly of fox hairs. Foxes are known to inhabit this very densely wooded part of the course and the birds had obviously discovered a ready source of this material. This just goes to illustrate some of the variety of material used in the construction of the nests and the lengths the birds will go to collect them.

Conclusions

The main question to be raised is, can all the time and material costs be justified? The answer from the survey undertaken at Ipswich Golf Club so far would be an overwhelming Yes, for three main reasons.

Firstly, due to the loss of natural habitats to urbanisation, hedgerow destruction and general 'over-tidiness' of the countryside, e.g. removal of dead trees suitable for nesting in, many bird populations are in decline. By providing safe nest sites, their numbers can gradually build up again sufficiently on one location to aid recolonisation of adjoining areas to occur.

Secondly, it allows local populations of small birds to be monitored. This can provide information on the effects of climatic fluctuations (see discussion of results) and put detail on perceived drops in number of a particular species within a site. This close attention can help in providing the correct management to assist the bird's recovery where necessary.

Finally, and most importantly, it is one of the more obvious forms of conservation management. As a percentage of the bird boxes are in full view to the Golf Club members, some naturally enquire as to their success rate. Initially, these tend to be the more ecologically aware people, e.g. members of the RSPB, RSNC, etc. Often the discussion about the boxes then widens to encompass how the golf course is being managed in general for the benefit of birds and other wildlife. These people, thus informed, then over a period of time interact with the rest of the Club membership and a positive message is conveyed. Hopefully, long term this type of public relations scheme helps to illustrate that golf and wildlife can co-exist in harmony on a site. The success of the nest box programme at Ipswich Golf Club is one excellent way of demonstrating this principle.

Bird Box Recordings

In the spring of 1997, Ipswich Golf Club trialed the British Trust for Ornithology's **Nest Box Scheme**. The aim was to provide more detailed data on breeding results in our bird boxes, not only for the club records, but also as part of a national survey for the conservation body.

Method

The scheme involves making several visits to each nest site over the course of the season. At Ipswich Golf Club this was carried out at two weekly intervals. Each check recorded the contents of the nest box as it developed from the beginnings of nest building right through to the fledging of the young.

At each box the time of the visit was noted along with information of nest construction, species of bird, number of eggs/young and stages of growth. The data were then recorded onto a card (available from the BTO) using a two letter code system, e.g. **AN** = **A**dult on the **N**est. To complete the record, details of box location and surrounding habitat type were also added using the same coding. Once the young fledge, recording ceases and the completed card is returned to the BTO for processing.

Results

There is no doubt that more detailed information about the actual numbers of young fledged from first brood nests can be gleaned from the records gathered using this scheme. Previously, only the percentage of boxes in use and the species occupying them was noted. By using this scheme it was discovered that great tits which were present in 13 nest boxes raised 99 young, whilst blue tits in 21 boxes raised a staggering 181 young. 280 young birds from 34 boxes – the course should be overrun!

Conclusions

The scheme was extremely useful in providing more in-depth data on the success or failure of nest boxes in general. For example, at one blue tit nest site seven young fledged but one egg failed to hatch; using our previous method of checking box contents only once at the end of the year, we would not have any idea of this success only that one dead egg remained and that blue tits had built the nest.

The main drawback to the scheme, however, is the amount of time required:

(a) to check 60+ boxes over 250 acres five to six times

(b) to collate all the data for each individual record card (grid reference, date, altitude, habitat type, nest build, egg number, young-growth stages, etc.) and encode.

Overall, it was felt that this scheme was an excellent aid to collecting information but took too much time and effort for it to be viable annually, especially as the survey period coincides with a traditionally heavy maintenance programme on the golf course. However, perhaps six to eight boxes could be targeted each year, with a full survey every five years to complement those findings.

N.B. Copies of The Nest Record Scheme Handbook and Record Cards can be obtained from:

The British Trust for Ornithology
National Centre for Ornithology
The Nunnery
Thetford
Norfolk IP24 2PU
Tel: 01842 750050
Fax: 01842 750030

Rudding Park Golf Club: A Case Study
By Chris Firth

The Site

Rudding Park golf course, an 18 hole historic parkland golf course, occupies the site of parkland landscaped by Humphrey Repton in the 18th Century and reclaimed agricultural land. It covers an area of 98 hectares, of which 19 hectares are woodland.

An ideal site for wildlife one would think, but during the construction of the golf course the wildlife was noticeably absent. Our first efforts were to encourage these back, which involved a substantial tree planting scheme.

Birds

Following several site surveys, it was established which bird species and how many each woodland copse could sustain to calculate the number and types of bird boxes we could put up.

The bird boxes were to support natural nesting sites to encourage the birds that we would expect to be in that particular site.

Different bird species have different requirements to be taken into account. The site and style of the boxes is important if they are to be used.

Site

- Out of direct sun
- Out of prevailing wind
- With clear direct flight paths
- No branches around the boxes to help predators gain access
- The larger the bird, the higher up the tree the box needs to be – 2-5 metres for small boxes, 3-8 metres for larger boxes

Style

We used the standard specifications for bird boxes issued by the RSPB in all cases:–

Standard: Small – with a hole of a diameter of 27.5 mm for coal, marsh and blue tits.

Medium: Hole diameter of 30 mm for great tits.

Large standard: Hole diameter of 32 mm for nuthatches and tree sparrows.

Extra large: Upper half of front section simply cut away to leave an opening suitable for robins, wrens and flycatchers.

Woodpecker boxes: We particularly wanted to encourage woodpeckers back into the area, so adapted large standard boxes to suit these birds by making a 50 mm diameter entrance hole near the top and then filling with polystyrene so that the woodpeckers still think they are drilling an entrance.

Owl boxes: We enrolled as members of The Hawk and Owl Trust to get specialist advice on creating better habitats and providing the right types of box. This followed a three year period when none of the RSPB standard owl boxes were used. We have subsequently erected six barn owl boxes and four tawny owl boxes to the design of The Hawk and Owl Trust.

Tree creeper boxes: During the recording of the bird boxes, we observed tree creepers in the woodlands so decided to try to encourage them a little bit more. We erected some boxes of a type recommended by the RSPB, and only after the first season of putting them up we are pleased with the results.

The boxes are a wedge shape with just a small triangular opening supposed to represent cracks and grooves that the birds look out for in the breeding season. Throughout wintertime, we noticed that wrens were using these boxes to roost in, so in real terms they have proved a success.

Installation

There are several recommended ways to put up bird boxes to avoid harming trees but on our site, because the trees were not going to be used as a timber crop, we used galvanised nails. Boxes need to be made out of wood at least 15-20 mm thick, some form of wood preservative (we used clear polyurethane varnish) is needed but must only be used externally with a clear surrounding area untreated so that birds enlarging entrance holes are not harmed. All the timber used to make the boxes was reclaimed timber from around the estate.

Finally, each box was numbered and all are carefully recorded.

Monitoring

After the first breeding season, all boxes were checked for occupancy. We could tell which boxes were being used by the debris below the boxes. Identifying the bird species is possible by the type of nesting material, old eggs or, in fact, dead fledglings. Finally, the boxes were cleaned out by removing any old nesting material – this helps keep down parasites.

Some of the boxes had been damaged by squirrels and woodpeckers expanding the entrance holes and repairs were carried out where necessary.

We decided that any unused boxes would be given two breeding seasons before being moved to a, hopefully, more suitable site.

Results over the last three years are encouraging and show that birds are returning.

Water features

Rudding Park has three existing lakes and five small lakes which have been created for the course. A programme of planting with native aquatic and marginal plants was carried out to maximise the wildlife potential. We now have coots and moorhens nesting and mallards visit. I have noticed that dragonflies and damselflies are now becoming more frequent.

One pair of Canada geese breed on an island. The population will be monitored because of problems that larger flocks can cause by fouling the lake edges.

Throughout the lakes and water features we are monitoring the reptiles and amphibians. Toads have bred in the deeper waters, frogs on the shallower reaches and newts breeding in the waters are able to move about due to the planting and management of the lake surrounds.

Grasslands

Changing the mowing regimes in the roughs creating variable grass heights has provided shelter and richer feeding grounds, bringing in small mammals, insects, butterflies, moths and, hopefully, ground-nesting birds such as skylarks.

Woodland

The woodland – eight separate copses – is mixed broad-leaved and regenerated copses. The site is bordered by woodland, hedges, fences and ditches.

We have extended tree planting schemes to create wildlife corridors for movement of wildlife but, at the same time, creating natural features for the golfers to play around on the course.

Future plans

Old mammal records show that harvest mice were once in this locality – whether or not they are still here we intend to find out.

Artificial nests using tennis balls donated by a local club are to be placed in suitable areas around the course in the hope of locating the mice and even helping to extend their breeding range.

These balls have 15 mm holes drilled into them ensuring only harvest mice can get into them and are then fastened to small stakes, each with its own number so we can keep a record of how successful or not they are over the coming seasons. Finally, each ball is baited with a little budgie seed.

We are carrying out an ongoing programme of small mammal trapping under licence to find out what small mammal activity we have on site. Once we find out this information then improvements can be recommended where necessary. Longworth small mammal traps are being used. A licence is needed when there is a possibility that shrews (which are a protected species) may be trapped.

Bat boxes

Bats are also protected by law, so specialist advice must be sought. We erected about 24 boxes as an experiment – three boxes per tree because bats need a summer roost as well as a winter roost. Local bat groups will be able to assist you with this sort of work.

Summary

All the works which have been carried out ,and all our future plans, take the commercial value of the golf course into account and, at the end of the day, proving that golf and wildlife can go together hand-in-hand.

Barn Owl Nesting Box at Loch Lomond Golf Club
By Abby Miller

Introduction

Loch Lomond is an area renowned for its stunning scenery and wildlife. Barn owls were once a regular sight on the ancient estates and farms that flank the Loch. Changing farming methods and a loss of nesting sites due to modern barn constructions have caused a decrease in the species throughout the UK.

The Loch Lomond Golf Club is situated on the west shore of the Loch, south of the village of Luss. During the summer of 1997, whilst working as the Club's Conservation Manager I was lucky enough to watch a barn owl hunting at dawn. The speed and silence of the bird as it swooped on its prey was breathtaking to watch and I was instantly hooked.

Many of the old out-buildings in the area had been renovated with a consequent loss of nesting sites. It seemed logical that a barn owl box would help resolve the problem. Providing a nesting box will only work if there is enough feeding habitat and our particular site contained many hectares of rough grassland which would support the small mammals that the owl would feed on.

Investigation

Having experienced it first hand, I was aware of one of the areas where the owl was feeding and a little bit of investigation soon led me to the sites where the bird roosted during the day.

Four roosting-sites were confirmed throughout the plantation and a pattern emerged. Our owl liked to roost facing south in trees that could be accessed easily from the outside of the plantation but never on a tree which was itself on the edge, always one row in. The bird showed a preference for parts of the plantation that had been heavily thinned and avoided denser parts of the forest.

One roost seemed to be favoured – a large collection of pellets (of varying ages) indicated a particular spruce tree in a plantation. Several hectares of rough marshy grassland adjacent to the forest offered ideal feeding areas, and the plantation avoided a sheltered nesting environment. I felt that this was the most suitable site for the box.

Some of the pellets were collected and dissected, the results showing that the bird fed almost exclusively on field vole (*Microtus agrestis*).

Choice and source of design

The box design was taken from Forestry Commission Bulletin 90 – Barn Owl Conservation in Forests (G. Shaw & A. Dowell). The A-frame structure has an 82 cm x 32 cm wide base, entry hole at the top and inspection hatch at the bottom. It was constructed from thick ply-board and covered with roofing felt to prevent leaks during Scotland's extended rainy season. Drainage holes were drilled into the base and I included a layer of pine needles to stop the eggs rolling around. It took less than a day to build.

Positioning the box

The constructed box was bulky and although it would have been possible to get it into the tree using a ladder on either side of the trunk, we found it easier (and had the equipment) to climb the tree using ropes and harnesses. This allowed us more freedom of movement and made positioning and attaching the box less awkward.

Although it is recommended that nesting boxes should face south to southeast, it was clear that the bird was accessing the tree through a clearing to the northeast. I faced the entrance hatch in the direction that I felt the bird could enter from its current flight-path. The box was placed approximately 3.5 metres above ground level.

Wire-rope seemed to be the most secure method of holding the box *in situ*. Two holes were bored into the back of the box and wire-rope was passed through the holes and around the trunk. The wire was fastened with U-bolts which could be loosened as the tree grew.

To help support the structure, it was positioned on a whorl of branches – this also helped take the strain from the wire-rope and prevented any damage to the tree trunk.

Once the box was safely placed, we removed all of the branches below it. Spruce trees can be quite easy to climb and I wanted to prevent anyone hurting themselves or disturbing the bird if their curiosity got the better of them.

Several of the surrounding trees were snedded to ease the bird's flight. The branches were collected and used to create brush-piles to encourage small mammals into the woodland.

External signs of interest

Evidence of success was soon visible, probably due to the fact that the bird had used this site as a roost. The presence of droppings on the roof indicated that the bird was spending some time sitting on the top of the box. I continued to find pellets distributed around the box and throughout the surrounding plantation.

Although nesting was not confirmed, the area was avoided from spring to late summer to prevent any disturbance, but throughout the season a barn owl was regularly spotted in the vicinity.

Confirmed

The first confirmed sighting of the barn owl using the box did not occur until the end of the summer in 1998 when I was lucky enough to notice the owl leaving the box at dusk.

Internal check

In December 1998 the box was checked and cleaned out. This job can only be carried out between the months of September and January to avoid any disturbance to the bird during breeding. A collection of white, downy feathers had accumulated in the box.

It occurred to me that the box was lacking one thing – a ledge for the fledgling owls. A young barn owl's first flight is rarely successful and they often have to "climb" back to their nest. I realised that some of the branches below the box should have been retained for that purpose.

The future

The barn owl continues to be spotted regularly (by everyone except those looking for it!). Fresh pellets in the plantation suggest that the bird has continued to show interest in the box during the winter season, possibly using it as a roost during bad weather.

In February 1999 I found an abundance of pellets under an oak tree only a few metres from the nesting box. The quantity and freshness suggested that the owl might have found a mate. Barn owls often roost together in early spring in anticipation of the breeding season.

This theory was confirmed a few weeks later when a pair of owls were spotted chasing each other and calling out, all part of their courtship.

With more than 8 hectares of suitable feeding ground within 20 metres of the box, the chances of successful rearing should be high. Hopefully, 1999 will see the establishment of a breeding pair in this nesting box.

Section IV

Appendix, References and Useful Contacts

Appendix

Simple Recording Sheet

Box Number	Habitat■	Bird Species●	Number of Eggs	Number of Young Fledged	Comments/Problems◆

■ **Habitat Types:**
  Grassland rough
  Woodland
  Woodland edge
  Hedgerow
  Near or sited in water

● **Bird Species (most common):**
  Sparrow
  Starling
  Wren
  House sparrow

◆ **Potential Problems:**
  Weather
  Predation
  Bird or mammal damage
  Nest abandonment
  Vandalism
  Other/unknown

References and Useful Contacts

References
Emery, M (1986). Promoting Nature in Cities and Towns – A Practical Guide, Croom Helm Ltd.

du Feu, C. (1985). Nestboxes, BTO Field Guide No. 23, 80 pp.

Useful contacts

The Bat Conservation Trust
London Ecology Centre
45 Shelton Street
London WC2H 9HJ

The Mammal Society
15 Cloisters Business Centre
8 Battersea Park Road
London SW8 4BG
Tel: 0171 498 4358

The Royal Society for the Protection of Birds
The Lodge
Sandy
Bedfordshire SG19 2DL
Tel: 01767 680551

British Trust for Ornithology
National Centre for Ornithology
The Nunnery
Thetford
Norfolk IP24 2PU

English Nature
Northminster House
Peterborough PE1 1UA
Tel: 01733 455000

The Scottish Ornithologists Club
21 Regents Terrace
Edinburgh EH7 5BT
Tel: 031 556 6042

The Irish Wild Bird Conservancy
Rutledge House
8 Longford Place
Monkstown, Co Dublin
Republic of Ireland
Tel: 00 353 1 2804322

National Federation of Badger Groups
Cloisters Business Centre
8 Battersea Park Road
London SW8 4BG
Tel: 0171 498 3220

For the address of your regional or county Wildlife Trust contact:
The Wildlife Trust
UK National Office
The Green
Wiltham Park
Waterside South
Lincoln LN5 7JR
Tel: 01522 544400

Turfgrass Titles of the World

The most comprehensive mail order book catalogue
for the Turfgrass Industry.
This catalogue brings together, from around the world, the widest
range of Turfgrass Titles available from a single source.
To request your *free copy* of "Turfgrass Titles of the World"
contact Margaret Richards at STRI.

Tel: (+44) 01274 565131
Fax: (+44) 01274 561891
E.Mail: info@stri.co.uk
or view our website www.stri.co.uk

NOTES

NOTES